Threadbare Like Lace

Second Edition
2004

Threadbare Like Lace

Jacqueline Baldwin (signature)

Jacqueline Baldwin

"Listen, children: do you hear the sound of the pine
trees singing? It is the wind, bringing stories.
I'll put the lamp in the window."

Grandmother Maggie Macaulay Mackenzie
(1882-1946)

Smoky River Books
Prince George
British Columbia

Published by:
Smoky River Books
1720 11ᵗʰ Avenue
Prince George BC V2L 3S8
Ph. 250-564-0572

Cover Photo by Lenard Sanders

**Library and Archives Canada:
National Library of Canada Cataloguing in Publication
Data**

Baldwin, Jacqueline Morse, 1934-
Threadbare Like Lace
Poems

ISBN 0-9735685-0-X
1. Title.
PS8553.A35T57 2004   C811'.54   C2004-906000-7

Printed and bound in Canada
by Papyrus Printing Ltd.

Table of Contents

Section 1V: *"Red Plates, Yellow Daisies, And Longjohns"*

Section V: *"Burning Bright"*

This book is dedicated with great love to
my three children:

Christopher Mackenzie Baldwin
Daniel Morse Baldwin
Morgen Tamarau Baldwin

Introduction

Jacqueline Baldwin, one of Northern British Columbia's talented new poets, has had poems appear in anthologies and won several prizes for her work.

In the past, she brought up three children as a single mother, operated an organic farm in Loos, B.C., near McBride, and ran her own accounting business. Until recently, she has had little time to spend on her writing.

Jacqueline was born in New Zealand, educated in private schools, and immigrated to Canada at the age of twenty-two. She travelled and worked in New York, Montreal, and Vancouver until 1964 when she started an organic farm at Steelhead near Vancouver. In 1969, she moved to Loos with her family.

She brought up Chris, Danny, and Morgen on the farm, which at first had no electricity or running water in a wood-heated farmhouse. Eventually the family was able to build an addition on the house, renovate the barns, build greenhouses, repair the well and acquire a diesel generator. She baked bread, preserved organic fruit and vegetables and sold and traded the produce from the farm. The family's needs were satisfied with the production from the land and the surrounding forests.

Jacqueline's poetry allows us a glimpse of what a pioneer life in the wilderness is like. She expresses deep love for the country and for Canada.

In 1991, she moved to Prince George to an older character home that is surrounded by trees and flowers. She named this property "Studio Dacha."

Readers of her poetry are impressed by her musicality, particularly by her ear for the human voice, and by her universal characters. The poems are a magical mixture of narrative and philosophy. She is a dedicated environmentalist and a champion of human rights. Her sense of humour, together with her great spirit and energy, and her determination to survive against all odds, are similar to the courage shown by our northern pioneers who settled in this beautiful, harsh country where temperatures can drop to thirty below zero and then turn almost warm the next day.

Her sensitivity and great affection for humankind show clearly through her writing.

Her characters come alive as she blends her experiences in the Rockies with her reaction to a pompous professor who grilled Betsy Warland during a seminar at the University of Northern British Columbia. Before Jacqueline's eyes, the professor turns into Marko, the family dog who is buried in the Rockies. The academic grows a long noise and pointed, hairy ears. His voice becomes the voice of "Marko Central," the voice Marko used when he felt it necessary to show his power and authority.

Marko with a shirt and tie
back from the grave
trailing roses.

Her ear for human speech, along with her fascination for the amazing old timers in Prince George is expressed in her poem, "The Victoria Medical Building" where an elderly man who has "seventeen year old eyes in an eighty year old face" comments:

goddam benches
facing the wrong goddam way
can't see a goddam thing out the goddam
window.

Another poem entitled "Reprimand" describes how one of the neighbours at Loos deals with the regional district bureaucrat when he demands that the farmer get a permit for his outhouse. The wisdom and humour of the poet and her character show clearly as Jacqueline explains:

The outhouse on Bill's hundred acres
had been in place for years.

The inspector insists that Bill must rebuild the privy according to spec-if-i-cations." Bill answers:

mebbe so, mebbe so
but at least I know enough
not to build a two-storey.

In the poem "The Good Sex Guide," an old pair of long johns are loved and worn until they are "threadbare like lace." The poem tells a wonderful love story set within the lives of the ordinary but extraordinary people who have the ability to laugh at themselves and who understand the real value of a deep, rich and binding relationship.

chuck it out, I say
no, he says
I am very fond of it
its tenacity fortifies me
encourages me
as I survey the impermanence
of life

The wonder of winter in the Rockies is again expressed in the poem "Silver Thaw" when, as the author walks "past the eddy" she notices that:

at the bottom of the hayfield
the gate into the woods is hung with icicles
the trees on the way to the island are singing

She is "captivated by the magic of the silver thaw" and "lost in a world of melting and freezing" imagining her ancestors sending messages across time as her kitchen fire begins to warm her.

Again and again we find that her images are clear and true to the country she has settled in as the picture of a "huge old cottonwood trunk" hollows out to allow space for her ancestors to sit and talk about their journey from Stornoway, Scotland to New Zealand in 1840.

In "Philosophy and Longing I" the author's friend from Australia longs for "the day when health, art, and education will matter and the military will have to hold bake sales to buy guns." In "Philosophy II," Jacqueline longs for a "chain reaction of gentleness" created by a "slight movement of air" that will enable us to become aware of "life's sweetness," of "wild raspberry mountain sunshine pouring down on blue, yellow, purple flowers" causing "our spirits" to dance "barefoot on the butterfly dream-wind."

Jacqueline's poem "I Want The Pipes To Play The Flowers Of The Forest" expresses her love for the human condition and sums up her philosophy with the line

it isn't dyin I'm scairt of

it's that life
this glorious bubbling untidy lovely laughing stuff
will go on
without me

So we will go on with the book and not miss out on the "laughing stuff" with its humour, its huge soul and its pain that has been, and continues to be, the story of one woman's life and work.

Barbara Munk-Buxton
Author of *Your Good Hat*

Section I:

Barefoot On The Butterfly Dream-wind

"Never does nature say one thing,
and wisdom another."

Juvenal, *Satires,* (c.100) 14.21

Philosophy And Longing – I

ancient mythical goddesses were believed to
assign one's fate
Lachesis designed the course of life
Clotho the spinner wove the thread of each life
Atropos, carrying the dreaded shears
scissored these life threads

we know better now
we have new gods
money
manipulation of minds
greed-speak
we even have new dreaded shears

management

we manage forests by clearcutting them
we manage oceans by mining them
we manage agriculture by growing food full to the brim with
invisible poisons
all in the holy name of profit

the poor
who used to have a social safety net
have now become
a safety net for the rich
who nod wisely
as they approve armaments budgets
rap our knuckles over the deficit myth
collect our money to pay for their excesses
then gallop off
tossing their glossy designer expense-account manes

a friend in Australia sent me a tea-towel for my birthday
blue border
bright yellow wattle flowers on each corner
and this verse printed in the middle:

I long for the day when
people will matter
when health, art, and education will have
unlimited budgets
and the military
will have to hold
bake sales
to buy guns

Philosophy And Longing – II

a geographer told me recently that a butterfly
in Beijing
lazily moving just one wing and thus creating a
slight
movement of air
can bring forces into play that could alter
weather patterns across the planet

hurricanes in Jamaica, cyclones in Canada, storms in Sweden
floods, death, destruction, land erosion
animals, fish, trees
gone

I long for the opposite
for the breeze that grows from the movement of the wing
to start a chain reaction of gentleness
awareness of our vital connections to other species
our dependence on them

a knowledge of life's sweetness
of wild raspberry-mountain sunshine
pouring down on blue, yellow, purple flowers
green leaves
children's laughter
clear flowing water
and sacred stones

and our spirits, dancing
dancing barefoot
on the butterfly dream-wind

C'est la situation tragique

the clerk at the music store says no
never heard of Gilles Vigneault
nor is his work listed on the computer
must be new is he?
Europe perhaps?
they have a different distribution system

carefully, we explain who
exactly, he is
how wonderful his music
how exquisite his lyrics
that we have listened to him
more than thirty years
in Canada

he is Canadian
from Quebec

a national treasure
an international treasure
one of the miracles of life, actually

Barbara and I walk on
down Central to the fish shop

she tells me a story:
a man, driven demented by his sons'
relentless playing of
rock and roll with the
volume cranked to the max
shouts at them:
please! can we have some decorum in this house?
is there no one here with a little culture?

grinning widely
his youngest son replies: well
here we are, Dad, with as little as anyone

next to the fish store there is a new video rental
emporium
we stroll in to take a look

the Canadian films in this
shiny
plastic
organized
sterile place
are displayed in an obscure corner
under a sign that reads:

"foreign"

Silver Thaw

my three children are
scrubbed clean and dressed for the world
by seven fifteen
porridge and fruit sticking to their
dear little ribs
lunches packed with home-made goodies

we walk out to the farm gate
through a world transformed
everything shines
last night it rained a little then froze
down to minus ten

after I walk back from the schoolbus
I decide to postpone chores
go down to the river
around the island
look at the trees

the sun is coming up red around Mount Ryder
I take the dog with me
walk down past the barn
where the cows stand, steaming
marking time
waiting for more hay

the latch on the cattleguard gate is frozen
I hammer it off with a stick
the dog races off down the track
chasing something

I walk past the eddy
snow has silhouetted the old car bodies
somebody put there in the forties
to stay erosion on the riverbank

at the bottom of the hayfield
the gate into the woods is hung with icicles

all the trees on the way to the island are singing
there are beautiful patterns on every branch
every twig
as if the world has been

dipped into an
ocean of liquid diamonds
come out sparkling clean

the sunrise now casts a red glow onto the trees
making the icicles blue, red, purple, green, yellow
giving them different music

red berries left uneaten by the bears
each one frozen with a
tiny peaked cap of snow
stand rebellious, audacious, brave

I am lost in a dream of melting and freezing
turning around and around as I walk
captivated by the magic of the silver thaw
on a whole forest of different species of
trees and bushes
coated in
gleaming
organmusic
ice

when I return to the house
the fire is out
I must tend to necessities
chop wood
stoke up a new blaze

I do this while still listening to messages
sent to me across time
in that symphony played by trees
painted with a sunrise

I heard this music with my eyes
the words were harmonious and clear:
we knew your grandmother when she was
a girl
we know who you are
we have been waiting for you

my fire is becoming stronger
beginning to sustain itself

in the flame I see an image
a huge old cottonwood trunk
inside which
my ancestors sit in a circle
talking about the six month journey from
Stornoway, Isle of Lewis, Scotland
to New Zealand
June to December, 1840

and how
compared to that journey
nothing could be cold
or lonely

ever again

Passionately Fond Of The Zamboni

in my hockey watching days
I used to love it when the Zamboni went over the ice
blotting out all the grooves, little holes, gouges
I loved what it could do

I want the Zamboni to fill up with its
sixty gallons of water and
come back
smooth everything over

let us have another
go
at life

like that game we used to have with the
tin hockey players

sometimes they would bend right over on the
tin ice
then miraculously be righted again and stand up

making a comeback

that's what I want
a comeback
after the Zamboni makes it all smooth again
we will all spring up
one by one
children, mothers, fathers
grandmothers, great grandmothers
grandfathers, great grandfathers
aunts, uncles, great aunts, great uncles

I want them all here

O Zamboni, Zamboni, Zamboni

I want them all here

for Christmas

Looking For Albert Almighty

I have been trying to re-learn how to live in the moment
instead of worrying, projecting
wondering if there will be social chaos
or if I should
paint the kitchen cupboards
so I bought myself a lego set
at Toy World
age five and up
built some structures
pulled them apart
rebuilt them
a fascinating, profound process

then took a jar of bubble mixture outside
blew bubbles in the garden
watched the kaleidoscope colours and the
floating orbs fly away, or
burst in a passion on the
red blooms of the geranium pots

Mischka the collie
one ear up, one down
looked on, puzzled

now here comes my friend from Montreal
Danilo
Professor Emeritus, Buddhist sympathizer
dear person whom I have loved like a brother for
thirty years

I pass him a spare bubble wand
we play a duet
on the still summer air

you know
he says
do you know that we

die

on each exhalation?

all we ever really have is just
one breath
the next inhalation

think of it
he says:

one breath

Five Wolves Up The Path From The River

in the early morning silence
warm air meeting frozen ground
left a grey mist hanging motionless
from the trees

I saw them walking
single file
past the ancient wooden barn
up the hill to the yard
through the fence onto the gravel road
that ran along the front of the house

belonging only to themselves
they walked slowly across my line of vision
from left to right
like ballet dancers

then disappeared into the bush on a trail we had named
the cranberry path

the first morning
I held my breath as they passed by
enchanted
spellbound by the sinuous movement of their bodies

it surprised me that they were not all the same colour
one was even
black

the next day I woke the children at six
lit the woodstove
bundled them up in warm clothes for our vigil

we kneeled behind the big double windows of
the front porch
waiting for the wolves to appear

my children
accustomed to wildlife
born to their own Canadian wilderness heritage
were as silenced as their immigrant mother
by the privilege of watching wolves so closely
without disturbing them

for three mornings we watched this graceful procession
this quiet deliberate pilgrimage
with gratitude and wonder

on the fourth day
we went for a long afternoon walk
in the sunshine
down the gravel road

a friendly neighbour from a few miles away
stopped to say hello
he showed us his newest acquisition

lying in the back of his red pickup truck was a
wolf pelt
complete with head

it was the black one

"my wolf" he said "for my trophy wall"

Bit Of A Bogguh All Roun' Innit

my friend John has farmed his
small piece of northern land
in Canada
for over thirty years

before the clearcutters arrived upstream with their
carpetbags

he used to trap, too, a little

in the war
he was in the British Royal Marines

he grew up in the house he was born in

a stone house five hundred years old
deep in the English country-side
on the northern border of Wales

you can hear the lovely rolling of those hills
in his speech
and in his serene blue eyes you can see what

five hundred years
in the same place
can bestow on a human being

whcn we were neighbours
he used to come over for tea
which he taught me to make properly
using patience and trust

one day there was so much snow it was
almost impossible
to shovel my way out
along came John on his skidoo
looked at the eighteen inches of snow
that had fallen overnight,   said:

a lot of snow, eh Jackie?
bit of a bogguh, innit

yes, John, bit of a bogguh alright

the day the 1990 gulf war began
my daughter was flying from Vancouver to Taiwan

I was distraught
imagining terrorists lurking everywhere

John was there when she phoned from
Vancouver airport
to say goodbye to me

don't go, I said
the war has begun
everything will be chaotic
I want you to be safe

she replied:
don't worry Mum
I'll be fine
Iraq is a long way from China

we talked for a while
she impatient with my fears
I in awe of her adventurousness

I poured John another cup of tea

I dunno John
this bloody war makes me sick
it is so wrong
my kids are wonderful people but
they no longer listen to me

in this symphony of the family
I am no longer the conductor

yes, said John, I know
it's a bit of a bogguh, innit
a bit of a bogguh all roun'

which, John?
which is a bit of a bogguh?
the war?
Morgen flying all the way to China?
the kids being grown up and gone?

well, said John
as his clear beautiful blue eyes look into mine

the knowin'

the knowin' about all this

it's the knowin' that's a bit of a bogguh

Old Husband's Tales

her mother-in-law had fifteen children
her own mother had eleven

at twenty-two
she already had three babies of her own
when she found herself pregnant again

it was 1939
just before the end of Canada's great depression when

money could not be found to help the poor
but appeared like magic to finance armaments

her husband was a good, kind man
whom she loved dearly
despite bone chilling poverty
the one room shack
in a remote logging camp

she found it impossible to go through with this

coathangers? knitting needles?
out of the question
slippery elm bark
herbs
quinine

something went very wrong
septicaemia, bleeding that wouldn't stop
the women caring for her promised never to tell

forever is a long time

her husband never remarried
raised his three sons alone
working the mills, the fish boats

the sons are in their fifties now
sitting around the campfire on the beach last summer
I heard one of them say to his grand-daughter:

lay offa them marshamallows, girlie
they're bad for your teeth

he turned to me and quietly said:
got a thing about teeth, I guess
because of my mother
she got an abscessed tooth way out in the bush
no doctor
that's how she died
nobody could save her
she bled to death
from an abscessed tooth

What Is In This Milk

Part One:

Gunnhild
the cow with personality
pure white
part Simmenthal, Charolais, Hereford
had a very powerful domineering streak

a non-compliant female
she ruled the barnyard and fields

we once watched her squeeze herself
at a wild run
through such a small space in a fence
we measured it afterwards
found it impossible
for her to have slipped through

perverse during round-up
disruptive when we were loading cattle
she would fling her tail in the air and
gallop away

even standing still she would look at us with a
baleful eye
that said:

watch out

I am unpredictable

get off my farm

Part Two:

she slipped on the ice late one spring
refused to allow treatment
wouldn't let anyone near her
healed it herself by
walking carefully around obstacles
taking no guff from the young calves
favouring her right hip when she lay down

while convalescing
she walked as if on tippy toes
exercising herself cautiously

back hunched, face set grimly
as if she were listening, listening for the pain

her whole personality changed
quiet, introspective
she communed with her body
aware of the changes in it

it was a relief to see her recover

resume her dreadful, defiant, old habits
her irritable, hot tempered behaviour
her certainty that she was invincible

Part Three:

I saw pictures of cattle on a news program last year
a new substance is being fed to cows in the States
bovine growth hormone

designed to increase milk production
by a chemical company claiming to know cows
better than cows know cows

a new way to extract more milk from a cow
who knows perfectly well
how much milk she wishes to give

the cows in the film walked the way Gunnhild did
all hunched up
tippy toeing about the fields as if
listening for hormonal changes silently coursing through
innocent bodies

they know something is up

this hormone is now being tested for use in Canada
to further enhance profits of chemical companies

Part Four:

O! spirit of Gunnhild
gallop away from these profiteers
toss your head as you
disappear through the fence
pass the word to the other cows

tell them all to turn tail and run away from
nefarious, dangerous, bovine growth hormone

when the profiteers try to catch you
stand there, glare at them belligerently,
tell them:

get off my farm

I Want The Pipes To Play
The Flowers Of The Forest

old rattle-trap green pickup truck
driving my little ones down the big hill to school
a wide-eyed neighbour boy
along for the ride
confides to me:

I'm awful scairt o' dyin'

didn't dawn on me for twenty years that
he may have been referring to
my driving

at the time I thought:
how profound
wondered if his parents noticed his six-year old sadness
talked with him about it
or
would it be natural
for the son of a big-game trophy hunter to think:

maybe me, next

I want to enjoy my own funeral
leave a lasting impression
as it were

difficult when you can't be there at the wake
cracking jokes
drinking tea
weeping and celebrating

it would be good to have on my tombstone
an inscription that is
different:

"I told you I was sick"

"What the hell are YOU looking at?"

I want a walking funeral with a Dixieland band
Saints Marching In and Wolverton Mountain
Danno and Morgen riding horses
Chris playing trumpet
women in long dresses
their hair streaming in the wind
dancing along with the music
glad they knew me
following a horse and wagon that will
carry my body

away

it isn't dyin' I'm scairt of

it's that life
this glorious bubbling untidy lovely laughing stuff
will go on

without me

Section II:

Back From The Grave, Trailing Roses

Hindsight

my husband gave me a green wheelbarrow for my birthday
then an axe for Christmas

it was what I wanted
a wheelbarrow for the garden
and an axe to chop wood for the fire

people thought it was peculiar
they thought perfume or chocolates
would be more appropriate

what would have been more appropriate
what would have saved me twenty years of misery
heartache and
devastating pain
would have been using the axe to chop him up
wheel the bits down to the river in the barrow
tip them into the current of that swirling water
dust my hands off
pick up the wooden handles
and walk back to the house
whistling

After The Honeymoon

so there he is
my husband
sick in hospital
behind locked doors
in a big dormitory with ten beds
which frightened the bejesus out of him
when he first saw it

I'm here alone with the children
hoping he will stay there
until I get rested up, which may take me
forever

this man
who promised to stick by me
in sickness and in health
and so on
has had the bloody nerve to become ill

I thought he was just miserable
didn't like my cooking
missed his mother
hated his job
or maybe
didn't like being married
after all

now, here we are
three kids under five years old
and father in hospital with
something they refuse to name

certainly not the kind of thing that can be helped
by serving him nice cups of tea
and smiling fondly at him
from time to time

I hear the doctor giving me the diagnosis
I see with my own eyes that my husband is
off in la-la land, and yet
hidden in this person is the man
I used to pine for
lust after
love

now he has become someone I have to take care of
for the rest of my life along with the children

I refuse to believe it, it is too serious
I cling to the remote hope that he will get well

meanwhile he is getting his instructions and insights
in directives from God via the TV set
which happens to be turned off

Are There Any Questions?

Part One:

Marko was our German Shepherd guard dog
until a couple of years ago
he caught something even the vet couldn't fix
and we lost him

my son Danno took him out to the Rockies
buried him in a field where his spirit could live near
snow capped peaks
and the wilderness

on Marko's beloved body Dan put twenty red roses
to take into the next world
filled in the grave
spread twenty more roses on top

our tears froze in the cold November wind

Marko had dozens of voices which he called up
to suit specific occasions:

joyful barks
running-in-the-snow barks
warning barks
welcome home barks
growl barks for the scent of bear

tracker-dog barks for moose droppings
baying to the echoing howl of the wolf
wild lonesome cries for the full moon

his speciality
which we named "Marko-Central"
was a very low throaty WOOF WOOF WOOF

often emitted when he was
too comfortable to move
too lazy to take a mad run at an imagined danger
but knew it was necessary to make some show of

dogness
to assert his masculinity
his power
whether he felt like it or not

just in case somebody was watching and
might think him remiss
if effort were not made to protest
something in the air that he did not quite understand

I think about him a lot
his myriad voices
his remarkable ability to instantly change persona from
loving companion to
snarling fanged guard dog

these gifts surprise me more now he is gone
than when I spent every day with him

loss does that

Part Two:

yesterday I went to hear the work of poet Betsy Warland
her presentation left me enveloped in a
dream-like cloud of happiness that
sometimes accompanies learning experiences

gently
she had bestowed a spiritual peace
that filled the room with a silence full of love
wonder
recognition

into this amniotic aura of reverence a loud voice
penetrated
the appreciative silence her work had engendered

his voice grated
rasped
dug ugly ragged grooves through the hallowed air

in a daze
still surfacing
disoriented
I forgot for a moment which realm I was in

I turned to inspect the source of this violation
as if the sight of his physical being could explain
this
shattering of my rainbow of peace
this
splintering into shards
the pristine crystal colours of her words

three rows behind me
a professorial person lounged in his chair
pontificating
directing what seemed
incomprehensible irrelevant demanding
questions at her
such as
who had influenced her work
was it so and so? or was it so and so? and what about
William Carlos Williams?

had he not been listening?
not heard her say:
"this is
me
standing on this ground"

then
it became impossible to hear him
as a new sound began to fill the room

WOOF WOOF WOOF

the voice of Marko-Central
WOOF WOOF WOOF

as the bullet voiced questioner
transformed
into a vision of Marko

WOOF WOOF WOOF
he said in that deep throaty growl
to announce to the world that he was
still in charge
superior
a powerful male dog
who could rip you to shreds if you weren't careful

WOOF WOOF WOOF
he continued as black and tan
bristles
rose up on his furry neck
and fangs appeared

white
menacing

Marko with a shirt and tie
back from the grave
trailing roses

making sure male presence is heard
WOOF WOOF WOOF
making sure we are forced to listen
WOOF WOOF WOOF
warning us not to forget

exactly where
and with whom
power lies

Listening To Daddy

tidal waves of piercing, brilliant, terrifying colours
clanging, discordant notes with zig-zag edges
crash around in the space behind her eyes
an alarm
warning her to close down

quick

before the sound of those words
his verbal abuse of her mother
can penetrate, become transformed into

meaning

the space behind her eyes is round
midnight blue on the outside
the surface thickly textured with white and turquoise

like remote snows in a distant land
protecting what lies underneath

she is too young to know the word identity
but she knows the mind-space is hers
that it is precious
must be guarded against invasion
by debris from tidal waves

alone
just a little girl
without asking for help
without confiding in anyone
she finds a way to make the words

and their exact meaning

glance off the ice-blue sphere
as a skimmed stone can be made to
skip
across the surface of water

Granny's Lament

saw the new baby today
red hair
blue eyes
tiny
defenceless
miraculous
breathtaking

thought of you
father of two golden haired laughing little girls
more than forty years ago
brought into the world by your so called love
for their mother

in that instant I imagined that if you ever

frightened this new child with your
rage-a-holic verbal assaults that
imprisoned our minds, I would feel like
killing you with my bare hands

this has nothing to do with hate
only with my painful knowledge of
what it would take to stop you

thank god you are already dead

Well, We Just Didn't Really Get Along, You Know

Dunblane reminds me of you

I have been unable to speak for the past two days
thinking about those people
their anguish
the permanence of it

that woman running
pushing her baby in the stroller, running
toward the school
not knowing whether her five year old was alive
or dead
reminds me of you
and what your madness did to me all those years

I saw myself behind that stroller
wondering
has he hurt them?
are they okay?
how will I keep them safe?

he is their father
not much help anywhere in 1969
it took me too long to un-believe
in sickness, in health, till death us do part

that little red haired girl, crying, saying to her mother
I can't stand it I can't stand it I can't stand it
as they laid flowers and teddy bears at the school gate
afterwards

made me realize why I hid the truth from my children
I didn't want them ever to have to live with things they
couldn't stand, couldn't stand, couldn't stand

not if I could help it

so I kept quiet

it all comes flooding back, twenty five years later
to reveal how much I hid from myself
laughing
while inside myself I lived in desperate fear
for all of us

this takes a toll on the psyche, I now learn from
psychology texts
for the first time I regard this elusive term: psyche
as something pulsing, like a heart
but without ribs and a breastbone for protection
it becomes bruised, scratched, torn, wounded
especially by lies and denial

it is time to tell

A Note On The Kitchen Table

it isn't alcohol I am against
it is drunkenness

I like wine with dinner
a toddy when I am cold
I love to share a glass of sherry
and conversation
with a friend at 5 p.m.

but what I can no longer stand is
the way you drink silently
hiding bottles
so I won't know you are drinking
pretending you are sober
when you are
barely able to speak
let alone think

I don't like pretending
now I am grown up
I don't like denying
the fact that you are drunk
just so you won't get mad at me

it disappoints me when I behave like this
a traitor to my own cause

what I really hate is to look for you
deep in your eyes
and find you
gone

What Does She See In Him

my friend and her husband
both of whom I have known for over thirty years
stopped in at my house for tea
hadn't seen them for ages

we sat in my beautiful garden
under the trees
surrounded by flowers and sunshine
drinking tea and talking

he refused to sit down, refused to have tea
paced up and down looking at his watch a lot
grumbling and complaining
while we talked about things that interest us
our children
books
economic practices
their effect on society

when she finished her first cup of tea he said
ok that's it, I'm going
you don't need any more tea and I want to go

she said
no, wait
we are in the middle of an interesting discussion

he said
you?
don't make me laugh
what in hell could you two have to talk about that is
interesting?
you are women
not only women
you are *old* women

nothing you two have to say could make any difference to
anything

believe me

in shock from the brutality of his words
I ushered them out

it took me a long time to get over this

eventually, despite lack of any apology
I decided for my own peace of mind
to forgive him

however
invite him back for tea?

not bloody likely

Section III:

Miniature Moon Goddess

Tough Little Kid, eh?

I woke up one morning
that first winter in the old farmhouse
went in to check on Danno, aged four
there had been a storm the night before
big wind from the north

the snow was fine and thin
so thin it blew through the wall
sifted in
through imperceptible cracks
onto his quilt

there he lay
sound asleep
snoring even
tiny little four-year-old snores
head and shoulders out of the blankets
and snow
real honest-to-god snow on his bedclothes

not only that
despite being in the room with him for some time
on his warm body
it still hadn't melted

Christopher's Cache

the dining room table was in a bay window alcove
overlooking lilac trees and
a hedge of riotous yellow
caragana

housework was not a priority

most of our time was spent outside
no time for excessive dusting and polishing

with one exception:

the bay window alcove with its window seat and sills
made of fine carved wood cut from a fir tree
grown on the property
over hundreds of years
growth rings so close they were
almost indistinguishable

one day
polishing this golden treasure with
love and wax
I found a little cache of dried meat
behind the royal blue cotton curtain
that framed the window

on examination
it turned out to be
liver

tiny pieces of moose liver
cut up at the table
slipped behind the curtain
one by one
forgotten
by a small child
who could not stand the concept of
liver
and chose not to discuss it

Sweet Dreams

but Morgen!
I remember you as a very sound sleeper
I don't ever remember you waking up and
calling to me
I said
mother superior
know it all
certain she is right about everything

my daughter says:

mother:

I woke up all the time in the night
terrified
but I couldn't call out to you because of the monsters
in the room who would then be able to pinpoint my
exact location
I couldn't blink
because that is when they would attack

I couldn't fall asleep in case my arm slid
off the edge of the bed
and that's when the monsters lying in wait
under the bed would
lunge out
grab my arm
and drag me off to their lair

sleeping was definitely out of the question

Sometimes You Live In The Country

I bought my son a budgie at the pet store
an adventure for both of us
driving the long road to Prince George in
spring thaw, early in the morning
milk the cow, strain the milk
get the others off to school on the bus
complete with lunches, homework done
clean clothes, smiling faces
then off we go
two hundred mile round trip to the pet store
his birthday treat
including a visit to the dentist for
expediency's sake

he chooses a bright blue female budgie
some bells she could ring with her beak
a mirror for preening, a bag of birdseed

all the way home he sings to the bird and talks in
bird-talk: cheep, cheep, cheep
he hugs the little travelling cage close to his heart

what will you name her, I ask him
as we transfer the bird to its cage in his room

Irene, he says, looking fondly at his new pet

every night when I go to sleep I want to say to her
Goodnight, Irene.

Playing House, 1977

sitting in my neighbour's kitchen
sharing coffee after a work bee at the community hall
one ear on the adult conversation
other tuned for my eight year old daughter
playing in the next room with four friends

Morgen, you can be the daddy
I'll be the mummy
the others can be the children okay?
you're the daddy so
the very first thing you do is
you come home
you bring your paycheque

what for?
asks my daughter

the four little girls laugh with delight

one of them patiently explains
well
you have to have a daddy who
brings home paycheques
else
how you gonna go shopping?

I hold my breath
afraid my small individualist will be dragged
innocent
into a morass of gender stereotyping
but she says:
no
I'm gonna go to work and get my own cheques
when I grow up
that's how I'll go shopping

there is no daddy in our house
let alone one bringing paycheques
for a few seconds I feel a mixture of
guilt, and sorrow
till I realize this wondrous person who is only
eight years old
just spoke her mind
while outnumbered
four to one

They Die Silently

Morgen was three when we began our
fish catching program
singing and laughing as we walked
twice a day down to the river
excited to see if there would be a ling cod
a trout, or if they would all be whitefish or suckers

difficult getting the bones out for the children
one hundred miles from medical care
no car to get there anyway
all possible precautions were taken
to avoid emergencies such as
a fish bone in the throat

we shared work equally
she had to do her part but
she could not bear the pain of seeing
or hearing
the fish being killed

she would run up the steep bank on her
sturdy legs
fingers stuck firmly in her ears
pleading:
wait till I have gone
wait till I have gone
then do it

she would keep her fingers in her ears
her eyes squeezed shut
until Chris and Dan and I
walked up the bank with the catch
tapped her on the shoulder and said
it's all done

now she is grown up, back home from
teaching English in China
travelling in Asia taught her more about Canada
than she knew before she left here

in Taichung, she said
there is a person called
the missing parts man
who goes each morning with a big truck
to pick up
the blind, the limbless, the paralyzed
whom he has bought
from their parents

he drives them to different corners where they beg
all day long
for money from passers-by

in the evening, he collects them again
takes all their money
drives them home so they can sleep
get rested for a new day of begging

he pays them a bowl of soup
keeps the money for himself
the missing parts man

they don't complain
don't know about exploitation
they think of it as an outing

she tells me this with her eyes squeezed shut

Whistler's Dog

my daughter is now twenty-six
a career woman with a degree in English and a paycheque
who wears business suits with mini skirts to conferences
and drives a fast blue sportscar

we went back to our old farm in the Rockies today
I am trying to find out why my heart still lives out there
in the mountains

walking up the road to the corrals
a good quarter mile from the house, she tells me
look! this is the exact spot I learned to whistle
when I was nine
I knew I'd got it right when Mischka

(the collie, who wasn't allowed out of the
house-yard, ever)

came belting up the road, ears back
running toward me
thinking I had whistled her up there

she walks over to the corral
climbs up onto the top rail and says:

you know Mum
that was one of my happiest days
it was such a great achievement
when I saw Mischka peeling up that road
I knew I would always be a really loud whistler

Springtime And Danny, 25

I took my son to lunch today
Earl's
twelve-thirty
Fifteenth at Central

he was on time for once
no sitting
twiddling my thumbs
wondering
where the hell
is he

we talked of Canada
of our passionate love for its
Canadian-ness
of women
of money
his lack of it

when I look at him I sometimes see
his four year old person
twinkling out of
my mother's New Zealand eyes or
her father's Scottish cheekbones

centuries adorn this Canadian face
tell me Celtic tales of the Outer Hebrides
of Maori canoes
of prairies
and the Cree, who were
long generations ago
his people

had I known then
when he was four
what I know now
I would have been a better mother
more serene
not so worried about
money
education
everything

I ordered salad
he had a beer

I watched him eat chicken fingers with
hot sauce

I didn't like the bill
twenty three dollars
plus tip

I thought:
that is a lot of money to spend on lunch

afterwards
as we stand talking on the corner
I remember another spring

sunny day
same corner

Fifteenth at Central

no Earl's then
 just a gas station

Danny is four
Chris six
Morgen two

thcy arc incredibly healthy
energetic
beautiful

calmly
 I say to Dan
"don't run ahead of us like that
you might get lost"

I don't tell them that I am
rigid with fear
of kidnapping
I don't tell them
as they skip happily along
that I am frantic
terrified
I have developed the senses of
a hunted animal

I don't tell them that we are
fleeing the madness of their father
who wants to kill us

I guess
twenty three dollars isn't much to spend
for lunch
when you think about it

Sunday Drive In August

I drive my son to the garbage dump in Prince George
my small black truck piled high with branches and debris
from the yard of his house on Hammond Avenue

where is this dump anyway and why aren't we
chipping these branches so we can
give them back to the soil or at least
use them for mulch
I hate throwing branches and grasses in a dump
it seems obscene
an insult to nature
a terrible waste
where is this place?

he directs me up Fifth to Foothills Boulevard and I think:
ahhh, Boulevard
the name suggests elegance
maybe going to the city dump won't be so bad

are we allowed to scavenge?
no mother, we are not
there are
rules

miles later
at the top of great hills
we turn left to enter the dump area

the smell is overpowering
a thick choking dust filters into the truck cab
even though our windows are rolled up

long before we slow to a stop the dash is
covered with a layer of
mustard coloured grit

we back up the truck and prepare to unload our
innocent cargo

big trucks and loaders roar about creating
huge dust storms
pickups come and go leaving things like
refrigerators
car parts
black plastic bags bulging with god knows what ugliness

everything, it seems, is to be thrown into a huge pit
where a machine will rev up, cover it with soil
and tamp it down

oh, comfort me with apples
for I am sick
of progress
I say to my son

he rolls his eyes

as we drive home he tells me about his planned
renovations
a hot tub will be installed, new carpets
fun will be had

I ask him if he has considered the
dangers inherent in
chemical components of manufactured carpet
he has not
I ask him if he thinks it might contribute to the causes of
cancer
he does not

I see he is relieved we are almost back at Fifth Avenue
soon he will not have to listen to me

I ask him how we can sit around in hot tubs
while the prairies are dying

he looks at me with affection, patience, tolerance
even love
and says:

Mother
we have to sit somewhere

Miniature Moon Goddess

Saturday afternoon
my daughter and one of my sons are here for tea
Chris has brought his daughter Mackenzie
eighteen months old

we three sit in the sunny room
talking and talking
watching my grand-daughter
invent a game for herself

there are more than two thousand books in this house
a few hundred of them within her reach on low shelves

her game keeps her busy for almost half an hour
she plays by aligning the spine of each book exactly
with the edge of the shelf
I am amazed at her ability to play so happily by herself
amused that she is making my bookshelves look so tidy
without ever removing any of the books

we are talking about the danger of diagnoses
how they categorize and stereotype people
and whether or not names should be used for
behavioural disorders
or
perhaps new names could be found that don't have
derogatory connotations such as
schizophrenia

I tell them my philosophy about our relative
that he wasn't really "crazy" at all
just got the wrong diagnosis a long long time ago
then treatments that made him worse

maybe it would have been better to call his behaviour
tennis, or elephants, or mandarin oranges
to prevent him becoming lost

confined in the name of his disease

at that moment Mackenzie tires of her game
walks across the room to me carrying with her the
only book she has removed from the shelves

solemnly, she hands it to me

written by Thomas S. Szasz, M.D.
it is called
The Myth Of Mental Illness

Section IV:

Red Plates, Yellow Daisies, and Longjohns

Grandfather Mackenzie, Storyteller

he told me stories that had great significance to him
made them part of my life-weave
threaded them through the fabric I was making
from all the mysteries
a child has to solve

later
when arctic winds blew in
bringing suffering and pain
it surprised me to find the stories were
wrapped around me
in that place where the heart holds the soul
for safekeeping

A Passionate Man

times were lean
they went to town only about four times a year

one day
in town for repair parts
grain for the chickens
basic underwear for the children
lamp mantles, wicks, kerosene
coffee, sugar, flour

she saw
propped up on top of a five foot shelf
in the army and navy surplus store
framed by sunlight from the window behind it
by white snow
and blue Canadian sky

an enamel dinner plate
made in Poland
bright red
with yellow daisies
circling the rim

she stood in awe
astonished by the song of the colours
wondering about Poland
spellbound by the music of red

in this cold winter that seemed as if it would never end
a winter full of potatoes and turnips
from the root cellar
ice on the drinking pail inside the house
frozen fingers holding the cow's lead rope
down the path to the barn

this plate

she turned the plate over and over
wishing she could buy it
dreaming of seeing it on her own wall

her husband watched her reverie

look, Jim, she said, look at this

he knew she was just admiring it
wanting only to share her delight
she would never spend a dollar ninety five on herself
he knew she would be thinking:
Jim works long and hard for his money
carrying a chain saw in heavy snow
wearing snowshoes
doing
dangerous work

she considered every purchase carefully
always weighing the value of the item
against the work he did to earn cash for the family

suddenly
he reached over
picked up the plate
and eight others
walked up to the cashier
plates held high

he put a twenty dollar bill on the counter
turned to smile at his wife

laughed loud at her expression of shock

she would have trembled buying only one

he bought them all

nine times the redness of one
nine times the daisies

still laughing
he bent down and whispered in her ear

the plates are for you
he said

your joy
is for me

Gyppo Faller On The Logging Show

my dear wife:
I am thinking about you and your famous feminist hero
Germaine Greer
who said:
"life is too tough for most people"

tell her I'm up Walker Creek
fifty miles from camp
there's twenty feet of snow and most of it is
down my neck and I am cold, wet, and
longing for home

the loader operator is new
he doesn't know how to keep track of our load slips
because the boss expects him to be a mind reader
refuses to teach him how
so God knows if we will get paid properly for our work

Pierre, his name is, and he has what
you would call an enchanting accent
but you should hear him when the landings plug up and
the boss is watching
the trucks lined up waiting for their loads are
losing money by the minute because
the loading goes so slowly

four skidders are idling at the edge of the landing
there is nowhere to dump their drags until
Pierre can catch up with the trucks

the truck drivers are cursing at him in
long foul sentences and
he, incensed by this injustice

his sketchy knowledge of English depriving him of
the luxury of swearing adequately, shouts back at them
doing his best to choose colourful, profane words
Eh! get your self up here! see if you do better, hey?
you…you…you…..bitches

at this point one of the truckers leaps up on the loader step
shouts threateningly to Pierre to
hurry the hell up or else and besides
don't call me a bitch,   you asshole

Pierre slams the loader window shut
glares at the angry face and gives him the finger
international symbol of contempt

neither has the energy for a fight
the trucker jumps off the loader step and walks away
his breath steaming into the mountain air
they really aren't mad at one another
only at a life that makes them work so hard
for money

this cold has to be experienced to be believed and I am
trying to fix my saw with thick gloves on
trying to pick up tiny little screws and attachments with
fingers that are cumbersome in frozen blue gloves

the shouting cheered me up, I thought I was the only one
hating this day, this situation

it is minus 38 degrees Celsius, nearly down to the point at which
Fahrenheit and Celsius meet
it is almost too windy for the fallers to work
almost, not quite
maybe they will wait till someone gets hurt
before they close down the bush for the day

I'm not sure if I can do this
I feel like crying
but I am forty two years old
expected to be mature
strong
manly
whatever that means

oh, my dear wife
your Germaine Greer person you are so fond of quoting, well
she is right
life really is too tough for a lot of people

Aphrodisiacs

the antlers guy is camped out at the fairgrounds
in a white five-ton truck from which he sells
fruit and vegetables
beside his truck is a sign in red lettering that says:

will buy antlers

I have an array of antlers and horns of various kinds
piled on the roof of a little shed in my backyard garden
elk, moose, caribou, deer antlers that I found
lying around the bush on our farm
they are here with me in the city because
I couldn't bear to part with them

they need a new home now
somewhere they can have another life
give somebody else the joy they have given me
just looking at them
listening to their stories

the antlers guy is standing in front of his truck
smoking a big cigar
I ask him about the offer to buy antlers
he says
I'm not buyin' today
showing me immediately I am in a buyers' market

what do you do with them?

he looks at me impatiently
as if I have no right to ask such a question
he says: I sell 'em, export, they grind 'em up

then he glares at me to make sure I realize he is
a very busy man

I stand there thinking about my lovely collection of antlers
their origins, their history, their life in the wilderness
the many moons they brought beauty to this earth
the songs of the mountain winds they have heard

no, I say
I do not like the idea of that grinding
they have special value as they are
they need appreciation
to be looked at and loved simply for themselves

the antlers guy wags his finger at me and says:

lissen lady, move your damn old truck outta here so my
customers can get in
willya?

Big Al's Buddy

Al buys himself a warm vest
feather filled
sleeveless
turns up at the sawmill next morning
seven a.m.
the envy of all

it's so damn cold this winter
nobody used to weather like this in November
minus thirty

they're all poor here
obvious enough
who else would work at this cut-throat place

his friend from Newfoundland says:

arrrrrr, she's a fine jacket you got there bye
whaddyu pay for 'er?

Al snuggles himself down into the warmth and protection
of the vest

ninety five bucks, he replies
plus tax

Lard, t'underin' Jaysus Al!
God Almighty!
that's more than a hundred dollars!

what would it cost, I'm wonderin'
if the bugger had sleeves

The Reprimand

the outhouse on Bill's hundred acres had been
in place for years
when out of the blue
in their wisdom
the experts at the Regional District Office
two hundred kilometers away
decided he had to have a permit for it

the inspector arrived in a fancy new pick-up truck
emblazoned with the logo of that governing body

this
said the inspector
will not do
you have no permit for this building

he opened his briefcase and took out a sheaf of papers
here is an application form you will need
and this is a pamphlet with
spec-if-i-cations
showing you how the structure should be built
it is called
a pit privy permit

well, said Bill, it ain't called that here
we call it the shitter
besides
it is already built
thar she stands
in use for years
even gettin' a bit full

Bill peered into the darkness of one of the two holes
yup, he said, she needs some lime

the inspector frowned:
it definitely should not have been built without a permit
people just do not know how to build properly without
our instructions

Bill rocked back on his heels
thumbs hooked under his suspenders
thinking:

mebbe so, mebbe so

but at least I know enough not to build a
two storey one

December The Sixth

my next-door neighbour is an artist
fashionably, left-bankishly poor
his downtown yard a mass of flowers
bushes
old trees, and
beautiful dramatic clumps of what are known
in some circles
as weeds

he sometimes brings me gifts
apples from his tree
cheerfulness
herbs
today he brought me a book of impressionist art
ten cents at the thrift store
I knew you'd like it
he said

I told him there would be poetry readings at the
Other Art Café
in memory of the Ecole Polytechnique women

he said:
you know, I couldn't attend last year's vigil
couldn't do it
my mother had just died
I felt terrible

so I stayed home and rang bells

yes
I could see him doing that
sitting there among his stained glass
his pictures
his books and dried flower arrangements
devastated by the death of his mother
needing solitude
ringing bells
brass and ceramic
reciting the names of fourteen women in Montréal

I thought of them, he said
as I recited their names

I rang my bells with each one

The Victoria Medical Building

I'm sitting in the lobby
on a cedar and wrought iron garden bench
waiting for a doctor's appointment that is
ten years overdue
when a man gets wheeled out and deposited
next to me
on the bench

he is seventy-five or eighty years old
thin, tall, stooped, gaunt, grubby
a nurse wheels the chair back to its place
and he begins to talk to me

"goddam benches facing the wrong goddam way
can't see a goddam thing out the goddam window"

charmed by this monologue
I turn to look into
bright bright green eyes
full of interesting depths
humour, sadness, intelligence, puzzlement
and pain

"goddam leg" he says
and points to his walking stick made of
twisted diamond willow
varnished
hand-made

"goddam doctors can't do a goddam thing
been in hospital ten days and still no better"

"I'm sorry," I say
still looking at his eyes which are ringed
with four or five layers of thick curly eyelashes
charcoal grey
seventeen year old eyes
in this eighty year old face

he grunts
I tell him I like his walking stick
that it is beautiful and shows
care and love in its construction

he coughs: Grand-daughter

into the swing of this conversation
enjoying it, feeling at home with him
by way of reply
I grunt

his taxi arrives, I help him
through the big double doors to the outside

as I open the door of the cab for him I see on his
baseball cap, this inscription:

biggest little whorehouse in Kamloops

The Good Sex Guide

a man on the radio is talking about underwear
not many people
he says
have enough fancy underwear
to last the week
a few days, maybe, is all
so
if you're going out and you think you might
get lucky
you take the good stuff with you

I do a mental rundown of my fancy underwear
count it to see if it would last a week
he is right
four days and I would be through my repertoire

torrid affairs are enhanced by fancy underwear
bras that give a distinct billowing cleavagey look
red satin slips
form fitting jockeys with interesting mounds
in the right places

under these circumstances
we do not wear comfortable old dressing gowns

to these occasions
we do not bring a favourite nightgown that covers us from
neck to toe and is a faithful companion on nights when
cups of bedtime cocoa warm the soul

I know a man who loves his most ancient set of
long underwear
so much
that he cannot bear to throw it out
even though the weave has worn very thin
and looks like lace

he talks to this long underwear as he
puts it on over his gaunchies:

"hi" he says "how are ya?"

when he takes it off
he holds it up to the light and
admires it, compliments it
on staying together one more day

he looks at me through it
tells me that looking at me through this underwear
gives him a totally new perspective about
us

he considers this underwear a work of art
he is proud that
despite having worn long underwear for forty years
this is the first time he has worn down a garment to
such a perfection of threadbareness

chuck it out, I say
no, he says
I am very fond of it
its tenacity fortifies me
encourages me
as I survey the impermanence
of life

he does a mock pirouette and
flings the long underwear up in the air

I laugh so hard with him that I spill

hot cocoa

on my flannelette nightie

Section V:

Burning Bright

Nalini's Feet

it's raining outside
Nalini shows up in a thick, beige windbreaker

from underneath this
shapeless, colourless garment
as she hangs it in my hall closet
emerges

a radiant butterfly
wearing an apricot sari

apricot

draped around her slender body
in intricate folds
regal
intensely feminine

through the pouring fall rain
she has walked from her car
in delicate leather thongs

a jewel shines on the strap
a diamond?
a raindrop
northern Canadian rain on this Bangalore foot

these are no ordinary feet standing on my hall mat
no ordinary mat, either
handmade
it came from the Tibetan Refugee Store
in Kathmandu

on the mat stands a determined woman

engineering degree earned in the years when
women didn't

especially in India

later in Canada a
Doctorate in Control Systems
in a language not her own

"how lovely you look!"
I tell her as I welcome her in

"I know" she says
smiling happily at all of us

her comrades

Backalley Sixties

he drove me from my office
to my rented house
where you were ill
resting
after your ordeal

it was my lunch-hour
you were at my house
so your mother would not know
what had happened

in those days it was illegal
we had to be careful
implicate no-one

least of all
him

unsure of his role in this drama
but
arrogant and patronizing
as always
he waited outside
while I comforted you
as much as I could
between twelve and one

then he drove me back downtown
in his red sports car
I couldn't speak to him
all the way from Kitsilano

he kept trying to be
nice
but I spat at him with my eyes
destesting his maleness
furious that his gender absolved him

hating his ignorance of the fact that
your love
your lust
for him
had made you a victim

I walked numb
unseen
through the basement of my office building
past the furnaces and underground machinery

I put the newspaper-wrapped package you had
given me
into a big gray galvanized garbage can

Getaway

I will kill you if you tell
he always told her

he said that every time
every time

she had no doubt he could kill her
after all
wasn't he powerful enough to
pin her body to her bed
so she couldn't move
hold his hand over her mouth to
silence her
surely, he was invincible

she wanted to tell her mother but
she was convinced he had
supernatural powers

she felt sure she would never get
the words out before she fell
clasping her hands to her chest
as utterly and mysteriously dead
as the Lady Of Shallott

besides, she thought it was
all her fault
everything
that there must be something
visible to others in her being
some indefinable thing that told them she was
bad

if this were not so, surely this terrible thing
would not be happening to her

so she taught herself a pretending skill
pretended she wasn't even there
every time it happened she waved her
magic pretending wand and
turned into someone she named
Samantha

Samantha had long black hair
Samantha could ride horses
white horses, bay mares, painted ponies,
buckskins, greys,
chestnut coloured beauties

her favourite was a palomino called Mint
whose mane flew in the wind as Samantha
rode through the night
under the stars
unafraid
free
across miles and miles of prairie grass
laughing

by the time she rode home
led the horse gently around the corral to
cool down
brushed its beloved coat
put it safely into the stall in the barn

he would be gone
she could return to her own bed
in which

nothing had happened

nothing

Recycled Bleach Bottles

early seventies
everyone in the community would pitch in
when a fire broke out
with whatever they could
labour, tools, trucks
acting quickly to get the fire stopped
before it burned out of control

my first forest fire
I had nothing to give except labour
at the end of a fire pump hose, and
the loan of my six bright orange water containers
to the firefighters stuck up on Johnson Hill
all day without water

the bottles were treasures
salvaged from the railway cookhouse
boiled clean
to carry water from the river to our house

six of them fit perfectly in my kids' wagon
six gallons in one trip
valuable items
precious cargo

to make sure the crew returned them
I wrote my name on the side of each bottle
not meaning any harm

my husband was spending a lot of time
away from us then
on his return
it upset him seeing my name on the water bottles

you wrote your name too big, he said
it makes me feel as if I am married to a
pushy woman

I told him he was married to a woman who had
no opportunity
to find any more such perfect water containers
a woman caring for three children under six
with no running water supply to her house
surely he must realize
the four of us had endured a dangerous forest fire

nevertheless, he said, seeing your name like that
in big black letters all over those bottles
knowing they have been used by
those men out in the bush
makes me uncomfortable
it dishonours me

I want you to

go out to the shed and
remove your name

I went out to the shed

painted clear varnish over my name

two coats

Totally Cool Super-Nun

I wonder if I could put into words how
lovely she is
this friend of mine
who is a nun

probably not
nuns are hard to describe

last summer she went to Newfoundland
for a holiday
took her aged mother along
they had a ball

one thing I really liked, she said
was that in Newfoundland I could
burn yoo-ees
and nobody tootcd at me
or got annoyed
they seem not as competitive or impatient
as we are
those Newfoundlanders

they seem
happier

what are you doing burning yoo-ees, I ask her
you're a nun
couldn't we have a little nun-like
polite, dignified behaviour?

no, she says, apparently not
smiles

at Saint Anthony's she stood on the shore
amazed
looking at the icebergs
a piece of ice floated in to her feet
she picked it up in
her two hands
looked it in the face and said:

hello
I wonder how old you are?

seven thousand years?
maybe just five hundred years?

she put it down gently in the surf

melt in peace, she said

Tuesday Night At The Popcorn Stand

I always go to Tuesday night movies alone
she said

my husband cannot stand to watch certain movies
such as
Trainspotting
Dead Man Walking

he is a very sweet man
with a tender heart
the kind of man who gets upset watching
Snow White and the Seven Dwarfs
what part upsets him? I ask

oh,
the wicked stepmother or
Snow White's supposed death
he gets all sniffly

I find it sad for different reasons
she continues
and that the time to cry is when Snow White
is expected to
and thinks nothing of
doing housework for seven men

Irreverent Laughter

hadn't seen Joanne for almost a year till today
Bay Day
mooching around the kitchenware department
this woman who looks like Joanne except
taller and thinner
comes up to me
gives me a big hug and says
yes yes yes
it is me, but I am ninety pounds lighter
I just love surprising people with my new appearance

the biggest change is on the inside, she says
where she now feels better
more at home with her own true self

I tell her how happy I am for her, how seeing her
looking the way she wants to be has given me
goosepimples right down to my toes

better watch them goosepimples, Joanne says
they will get you into trouble and by the way

one of the biggest benefits of losing all that weight
is that I can now get my knees up around my ears
during lovemaking and let me tell you I
sure missed that all those years I was so heavy

Joanne always made me laugh a lot
even as she begins to tell me about her stepfather
the same one who abused Jo and her sisters

they always hoped their Mum would leave but
all they could do was get the hell out
as soon as they could look after themselves

he's dead you know
died just a year ago in his sleep

Joanne does not look sad
her eyes twinkle and she laughs as she goes on:
Mum was combing her hair, getting ready for church
she was looking in the mirror at his reflection
lying there in their double bed, thinking:

he looks funny
wonder what the hell is wrong with him now

the doctor said he had been dead all night
Mum didn't even notice! how about that?
Saturday night and she still didn't notice he was dead
Joanne cracks up laughing

we went to the funeral for Mum's sake only
all of us, all the sisters

it was hard listening to the minister praise the dead

when they lowered the coffin into the ground
I just couldn't help it, I whispered to my sister:
I don't suppose it would be appropriate for us to

dance now would it?

Augusta

I'm not into that old lady stuff, she says

Augusta is seventy
lives alone except for
Kenmore, her red cat

she has wispy grey hair that flies off in
all directions
she doesn't knit
or quilt
nor does she smile at babies
to whom she is more likely to read
a little Voltaire, saying:
a classical education
begins
at the moment of conception
this baby
has some catching up to do

Augusta is studying art history
walks over to the college
wearing bright blue leg warmers
pink jogging suit
runners
muttering
listening to Dwight Yoakum
on her earphones which she calls her
walk-person

she says that isn't Dwight's real name
he just adopted it so he would sound more
country

her four grand-daughters
busy with boys
lipstick
spiral perms
are embarrassed by her pronouncements
in front of their friends
but

alone with her
the five of them laugh and laugh
yesterday she said to them:
after this crazy dam-fool
mating season of yours is over
you won't think I am such an oddball
you might even
walk in my footsteps

if you're lucky

Hanging In

she phones from New Brunswick to tell me
she hasn't heard from him since spring
he's vanished into thin air
somewheres near Prince Albert, Saskatchewan
last she heard

winter is coming on and the kids need
clothes
schoolbooks
and God! don't even mention Christmas

she has two jobs, twelve hours a day
nets eleven hundred a month

but the rent is seven fifty
which doesn't leave much for food or
busfares, heat, medical, dental, toys,
hope

I can't make it anymore, she says
it isn't enough for the four of us
I hardly ever see the kids, and even when I do
I am so frigging tired
I fall asleep reading stories to them

tell me what you need, I say to her
tell me what I can do

send me fifteen bucks
I want to get my eyelashes tinted
down at the beauty salon
all this crying keeps smudging my mascara

Chivalry

seventeen
walking home in the dusk from piano lessons
she turned the corner of her street

lights unseen since the beginning of the war
shine out in the frosty air
a welcome from every window
outlining the bare trees in the garden
the brick fence
iron gate

it didn't occur to her to be apprehensive

chaos met her
entrance hall full of german soldiers
drunken laughter
polished boots

someone grabbed her
tossed her like a rag to the
centre of the room

she screamed for her mother
her father
the servants

nobody answered

next morning she escaped
through the back hall
down the cellar stairs
over the orchard fence
dripping blood
shame
fury

in her mid-seventies now
she lives in a retirement home
in a quiet northern Canadian town

a terrifying presence to the other residents
her loud voice
outspoken views
shaking her clenched fist at the television
shouting
liars! hypocrites! bastards!

in the visitors lounge she shocks guests by
announcing that she is a murderer
they don't believe her

it is beyond the imagination of
these kind, good people who have lived all
their lives peacefully in a rural parish
that this wild-eyed woman with
thick, straight, white hair could have
lived in a sewer during the war
from the age of seventeen
a woman who claims to have
killed every german soldier she could
get her hands on

they look at one another
tap their temple with a bent finger
signifying their confirmed opinion that she is
not to be taken seriously

they prefer to think of her as
one of the crazies

an elderly gentleman
convinced he is the only one who still has
all his marbles
pretends he is on the phone

an old wooden wall-model

with his left hand holding a make believe
black trumpet receiver
he rings the wind-up bell with his right hand

he doesn't know about cellular phones
how easily they fit into a pocket now
he uses the old ways
places the receiver against his left ear
rings the bell with the imaginary handle

hello central? he says
this is 39M
hello central?

he is phoning for help
phoning central
to call for help for that
seventeen year old girl
fifty seven years ago
somewhere in Poland

hello central?
this is urgent

he rings the hand turned bell again and again
eyes glued to the imaginary walnut panels
of the imaginary wallphone

Nellie

the doctors love Nellie
she cheers them up

tells them not to bother with her
her broken hip will heal, or it won't

she laughs, waves them away
go tend to people who are really sick

one quiet afternoon
she tells us her philosophy of women's lives:

don't know what it's like now
maybe worse, but
back in my day
men were always after women

it was amazing and frightening
you could read it in their eyes
being in the same room with them made me
uncomfortable, scared
because of their air of power, violence

you mean sex, we said

no, I don't mean sex
I was married to my husband for thirty eight years
before he died
never once did I see in his eyes what I saw
in other men, starting with my father
all my uncles, even my brother
it was as if they were possessed by
something uncontrollable
that could only be remedied by
my body

oh, I got sick of it
always letting my eyes glaze over the
obviousness of it
pretending I didn't notice

I escaped as soon as I could to a
good loving man
a man who equated sex with love and respect

these young nurses feel sorry for me because I am
seventy four, grey hair, wrinkles
not long to live
also I have this broken hip
might not be able to walk again

but, you know
I couldn't endure what they have to
always being the target of someone else's needs

I'd rather have my simple life
my books, my friends, my memories
you can't imagine what a relief it is
not to have to deal with that constant, awful
desire

For The Love Of Glenda

sticks and stones may break your bones
but words
will never hurt you

I didn't understand that one
when I was little
it only taught me that I was wrong
and they were right
as usual

only wimps
who would never become
good soldiers

could be slain by the impact of words

today in the mail comes
a newspaper clipping

from my friend in Sun Valley
a death notice
her lover died suddenly in late December
forty five years old
massive heart attack
four o'clock in the afternoon
leaving her
without him
the major factor in her world
a primary column in her Grecian mansion
built stone by stone over more than twenty-two years

the notice says:
Gary is survived by Glenda
his long-time

paramour

the sight of the word paramour
overwhelms me
leaves me weeping
wild ancient wailing tears

there seems no end to the terrible grief that
covers me like a thick web of
foggy prehistoric sadness

why didn't I feel this kind of grief when she
called me four weeks ago in December?
how was I able to remain calm
comfort her
assure her of my endless love and support
how?

I knew then how much she loved him
I knew he was dead
I knew she was bereft

but I did not know this word

I look it up
under "P"

my hands are shaking so much I can hardly lift
volume two
of the *New Oxford Shorter English Dictionary*

paramour

the definitions take up three inches of space in
one column
illustrate the subtle nuance hidden in English words
the many meanings attributed to one word

the literal translation from French
"par amour"
seems most fitting for my Glenda

by
or through
love

yes, by, or through
or both

paramour

it signifies the spirit of Glenda
a woman who did not believe in marriage
for herself

a woman who defied convention
chose a much younger man
for a lover
twenty two years ago

in the days when
it was an act of resistance against society
its colonialist rules
its hatted and gloved tut-tutting
born of the purse lipped fifties

long-time : *paramour*
a word with orange and yellow in its purple hills

the shock is wearing off
becoming replaced by a deep understanding of
the immensity of her loss
and the intensity of my own love for her
whom I have known for thirty five years

the word has sliced me through to the bone
lain bare the false ideals of propriety
to reveal Glenda as she is

a woman honouring life
by living it
by,
or through,

love

Acknowledgements:

Some of the poems in this collection have appeared in anthologies: *Chips From The Block, 1993,* and *Anthology Ninety Four*. "Nalini's Feet" appeared in *Asterisk*, the Faculty Association Journal of the College of New Caledonia; "Springtime and Danny, 25, in the Central Interior Regional Arts Council publication: *Arts North;* and "After the Honeymoon" in the *Writers' Bloc Journal.* Other poems have been published in the *Westjet Inflight Magazine, Connections Magazine, Guide to the Goldfields, Reflections on Water, It's Still Winter,* and read on CBC radio on *Richardson's Roundup, North By Northwest, This Morning, The Vinyl Café, and Arts Today.* "Passionately Fond Of The Zamboni" has been accepted for publication by the British Columbia Ministry of Education for their Grade 12 English examinations, and also won a place on British Columbia's *Poetry In Transit.* The book reached the British Columbia best-seller list in 1998, won honourable mention for the Laura Jamieson prize awarded by the Canadian Institute for the Advancement of Women in 1999, and won the Jeanne Clarke Memorial History Award in 2000. *Threadbare Like Lace* has been chosen as a classroom text in English at the University of Northern British Columbia, the Mackenzie High School, and the College of New Caledonia. This Second Edition of *Threadbare Like Lace* is its sixth printing since the book was launched in 1997.

I am grateful to poet and editor the late Barbara Munk, and to classmates and teachers at the University of Northern British Columbia for their interest in my writing. My thanks to Professors Marika Ainley, Karin Beeler, Rob Budde, Julia Emberley, Jo Fiske, Kevin Hutchings, Dee Horne, Antonia Mills, Si Transken, Lynda Williams and Larry Woods, for their inspiration and encouragement. Special thanks to Susan Hunter of the College of New Caledonia.

I want to gratefully acknowledge all those readers who write to me about *Threadbare Like Lace,* to tell me about their own lives, and to discuss their responses to my poems. Their beautiful letters, e-mails, and telephone calls are treasured and appreciated.

A great number of people are involved in the process of writing and publishing a book. I thank my many helpful and enthusiastic muses and mentors:

Michael Armstrong, Lisa Aubrey, Morgen Baldwin, Jim Brinkman of Books and Company and Café Voltaire, Joan Buchanan, Harvey Chometsky and Lilla at the old Other Art Café, Dale and Neil at the Northern Society of Musicians and Artists, Laurell Crocker, Mary-Lou Curtis, Daniel and Betty Dorotich, Shirley Dumas, Christopher Earl, Doreen Fowlston, Chuck Fraser, Marylin Hannah, Christine Jackman, Shirley Lehovich, Han Li, Lynne Van Luven, Joy and Bob McKellar, Linda Morse, Diane Nakamura, Maureen Nicol, Frank Peebles, Brenda and Mark Roland of the Rae King Blues Band, George and Bridget Sipos of Mosquito Books, Patricia and John Smith, Helen Stewart, Joanne Stuart, Anne Tiffany, Allen Waldron, Cynthia Wilson, and in respectful memory: the late and beloved Bob Harkins, Bridget Moran, and Lynne Smith.

My thanks to those in the extraordinarily vibrant community networks that flourish in and around Prince George, British Columbia, in support of creative endeavour, for inspiring me to seek and find my own voice in poetry.

Jacqueline Baldwin, 2004

Praise for Threadbare Like Lace:

"We close our program with a singularly Canadian poem by Jacqueline Baldwin of Prince George, British Columbia: *Passionately Fond of the Zamboni*."

Eleanor Wachtel, *The Arts Today,*
CBC Radio, Toronto

"*Threadbare Like Lace* – reflective poems reminiscent of many of the Black Mountain poets."

The Vancouver Sun

"Baldwin is capable, as in *Listening To Daddy,* of fusing sufficient tenderness, anger, and psychology to sweep away insignificant detail, (her work) is often relieved by a strongly comic or satiric impulse."

Gary Geddes, British Columbia Bookworld

"Her poems tell stories. Simple everyday situations are painted with a creative brush. She finds the angle which enlightens us, allows us to appreciate humanity as we struggle to make sense of our world."

Sharon Stearns, The Sentinel, Valemount B.C.

"This book has become a legend."

The Milestones Review

"Jacqueline Baldwin is what this country is in short supply of: a good gateway poet into the deep dark Atwoods. She embraces the same sensitivities, the same issues as Margaret Atwood et al but does it with a deliberate low brow. Simplicity is what turns these pages. She tells quaint and comic poems about Zambonis and underwear."

Frank Peebles, The Free Press, Prince George B.C.

"Jacqueline Baldwin's ability to express sophisticated thought and complex ideas in a highly accessible language will ensure that this volume will inspire, educate, and move generations of readers."

Marianne Gosztonyi Ainley, PhD
Adjunct Professor of History, UNBC
Adjunct Professor of Women's Studies,
University of Victoria, B.C.

"A storyteller of the highest order, Jacqueline's gift enables readers to share in the clarity of her vision as she sifts through the weave of human experience."

Chaff Magazine, Massey University, New Zealand

"I flipped it open [*Threadbare Like Lace*] at random and I read a poem called "Whistler's Dog". It made me smile. I bought the book."

Stuart McLean, The Vinyl Café, CBC Radio

List of Writing Awards:

(1) <u>Central Interior Community Arts Council</u> (CIRAC) Literary Contest: 1993:   Third Prize, Poetry Division, for *"After The Honeymoon"*

(2) <u>Central Interior Community Arts Council</u> (CIRAC) Literary Contest: 1994:   Second Prize, Poetry Division, for *"Springtime and Danny, 25"*

(3) <u>Central Interior Community Arts Council</u> (CIRAC) 1996: First Prize, Poetry Division, for *"The Good Sex Guide"*

(4) <u>Canada Council for the Arts *Poetry In Transit* Contest, Vancouver</u> 1997:   Place on BC Transit Bus and Skytrains for *"Passionately Fond of The Zamboni."*

(5) <u>Canadian Research Institute For The Advancement Of Women, Ottawa</u> 1999:   Honourable Mention for the English Prize: Laura Jamieson Prize, awarded to the best feminist book, by a Canadian author, which advances knowledge and/or understanding of women's experience.   For *"Threadbare Like Lace."*

(6) <u>Woman of Distinction Award for Arts and Culture, Northern British Columbia</u> 1998:   For *"Threadbare Like Lace"* and contribution to the Arts Community in Northern British Columbia.

(7) <u>Torrefazione International Poetry Competition, Seattle, Wa.</u> 1999:   First prize out of 200 Vancouver section entries for poem: *"Chiaroscuro."*

(8) <u>Prince George Public Library Jeanne Clarke Memorial Local History Award</u> 2000:   For outstanding service in the field of local history for *"Threadbare Like Lace."*

(9) <u>Men Against Violence Against Women Committee</u>, and Prince George Violence Against Women In Relationships Committee: 2001:   Hazel White Award of Courage.   Re: non-fiction poem/essay: *"Contempt Of Court."*

(10) Inducted into the *Arts Gallery Of Honour, 2007,* of the Prince George and District Community Arts Council for her contribution to Literary Arts.

(11) Honoured by inclusion in The University of Northern British Columbia's Northern Women's Centre *"Women's Wall Of Fame"* for her contributions to the Centre through her writing and public readings of her work at University events.

(12) *Threadbare Like Lace* sold out its first printing in three weeks in October 1997, and earned a place on the British Columbia Non-fiction Bestseller List in Spring, 1998.

About the Author:

Born and educated in New Zealand, Jacqueline Morse Baldwin immigrated to Canada at the age of 22, travelling and working in Montreal, Vancouver, Banff, the Laurentian Mountains, and at United Nations in New York City.

After raising her three children on a wilderness organic farm in the Canadian Rockies, she moved to town to a beautiful, old, tree-surrounded house she named "Studio Dacha" in downtown Prince George, British Columbia, to return to school and pursue her interest in writing. Caitlin Press has published two volumes of her poetry: *Threadbare Like Lace (1997)* and *A Northern Woman (2003),* her work has appeared in journals and anthologies, and in the web journals *Reflections On Water* and *It's Still Winter.*

Jacqueline has performed over 400 public readings of her work including on CBC radio and television programs, and in Elementary, High School, and University classrooms. She has read her poems to audiences in convention hotels, civic centres, blues bars, art galleries, libraries, Fringe Festivals, riverside flower ceremonies, weddings, funerals, coffee houses, bookstores, theatres, hospitals, village halls, on a British Columbia Ferry boat stranded in a snowstorm, at December 6th Memorial Services, Jezebel's Jam concerts, to passengers on a cross Canada train, in churches, jails, and at the "Learn-to-Earn School for Bartending." Her biography appears in *The Who's Who of Canadian Women, (1998) and in the Canadian Who's Who, (2000).*

She sings the praises of this Northern city, which is extraordinarily supportive of the arts, music, theatre, dance, and education. She finds it a privilege to live among people who are so deeply committed to building and maintaining a strong sense of community.